WHY SETTLE FOR A SLICE, WHEN YOU CAN HAVE THE WHOLE PIE!

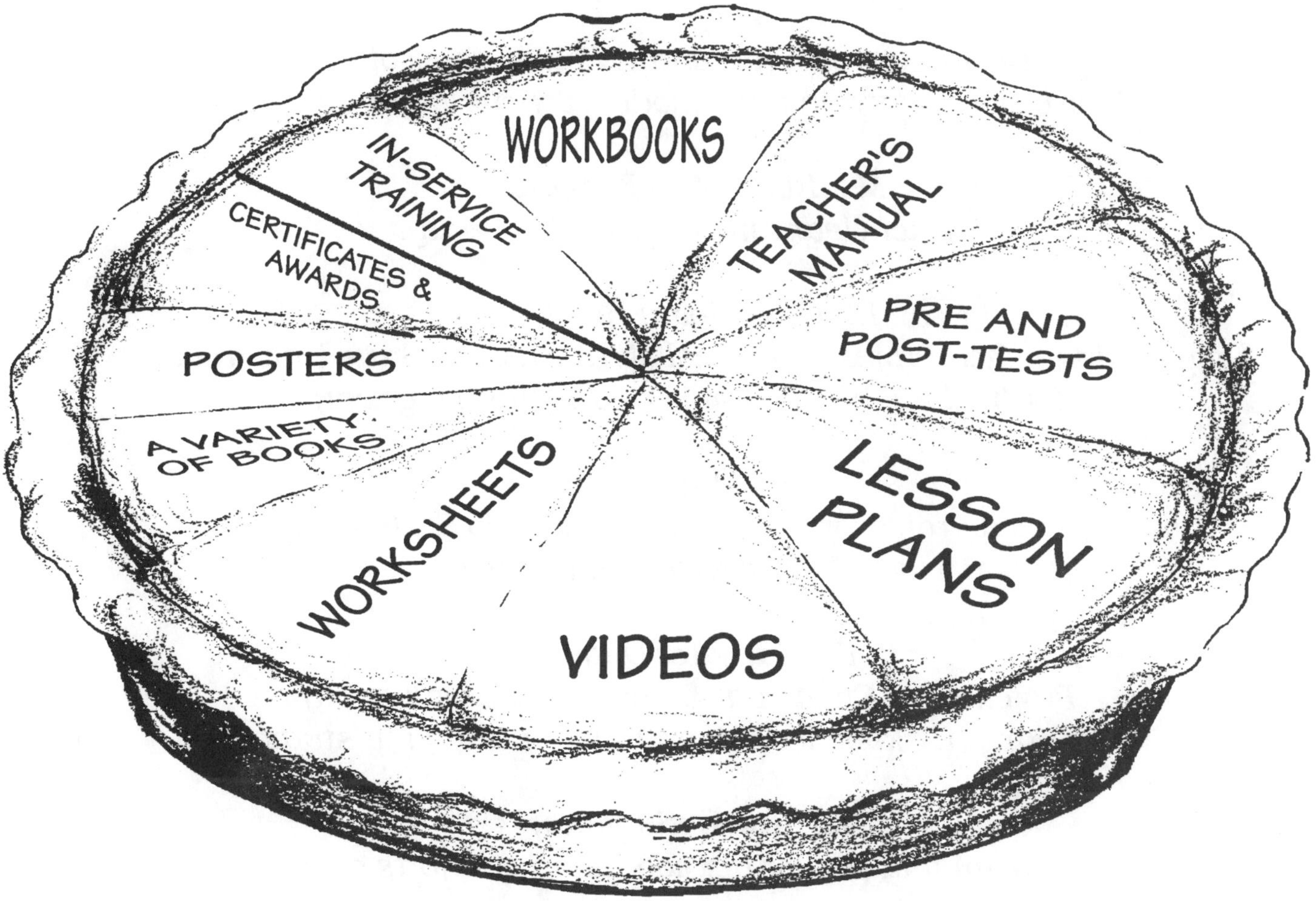

WORKBOOKS
TEACHER'S MANUAL
PRE AND POST-TESTS
LESSON PLANS
VIDEOS
WORKSHEETS
A VARIETY OF BOOKS
POSTERS
CERTIFICATES & AWARDS
IN-SERVICE TRAINING

The workbooks are designed for K-12 and are a very important component of SETCLAE's comprehensive, Africentric, multicultural curriculum.

ACKNOWLEDGMENTS

I would like to thank the following individuals for their contributions in making this workbook possible:

Dr. Jawanza Kunjufu and Folami Prescott,
for their vision in creating this model curriculum for our youth.

Ms. Rita Smith-Kunjufu,
for her clear directions and serenity.

Dr. Gwendolyn Brooks,
my distinguished Professor of English at Chicago State University,
for holding the torch high and lighting my way.

Haki Madhubuti,
my esteemed Professor of English at Chicago State University,
for being an excellent teacher.

Dr. Margaret Duggar,
Professor of English at Chicago State University
for sharing her knowledge and humor during my studies.

Ms. Kimberly Vann,
African American Images, for her coordinating efforts and patience.

Ms. Adrian Payton-Williams,
African American Images, for her technical support.

Ms. Charlene Snelling,
Resource Librarian, Chicago State University for her encouragement and finally, the Creator of the Universe without whom nothing would exist.

Doriel R. Mackay, M.A.

SETCLAE

Self-Esteem Through Culture Leads to Academic Excellence

2nd Grade Workbook

Harambee Sessions Illustrations by Reginald Mackey

First edition, first printing

African American Images
Chicago, Illinois

THE SETCLAE WORKBOOK
SECOND GRADE
TABLE OF CONTENTS

INTRODUCTION

HARAMBEE SESSIONS

INTRODUCTION

Jambo mwanafunzi (Hello students)! Welcome to SETCLAE! This program was designed to help you achieve excellence in your studies in school by making you aware of:

Your history
Goals to strive towards
Helping you to achieve self-esteem
Developing love for your family, friends, classmates and community.

In each Harambee Time (lesson), the symbol (HG) will let you know when you'll be working with your Harambee Group. The symbol is found next to the word Materials. It is our hope, we teachers (mwalimu), that as we try to impart this knowledge to you and share some basic principles with each other that we both shall grow. These principles are:

Umoja - Unity
Ujima - Collective work and responsibility
Ujamaa - Cooperative Economics
Nia - Purpose
Kuumba - Creativity
Imani - Faith
Kujichagulia - Self-determination

So, HARAMBEE (Let's Pull Together) for together we shall win!
Pamoja Tutashinda!!

Enjoying the Benefits of SETCLAE

Here are some tips to help you enjoy the benefits of SETCLAE:

1. Be an active Harambee Group member! Complete the assignments. Ask questions. Help members of your group who don't learn or work as quickly as yourself.

2. Be creative! When coloring materials are needed, use a variety of materials including markers, paints, crayons, tissue paper, whatever you can get your hands on.

3. Be original! Use your ideas to create poems, raps, skits, songs, dances, dramatic presentations, speeches, plays, books, articles, and letters to share your insight with others.

4. Be encouraging! When working in Harambee Groups, encourage members to take on tasks based on their talents and interests. Each group should identify someone to fulfill the following roles:
   Group Leader
   Artist
   Rapper/Poet
   Observer
   Of course, one person can perform several of these roles simultaneously.

5. Always remember: everyone is a "mwalimu mwanafunzi" (teacher and student).

6. Never forget what SETCLAE stands for: Self-Esteem Through Culture Leads to Academic Excellence.

To get the full benefits from this workbook, you will be using it as just one component of the SETCLAE program. If you are using it exclusively, you will need to have the following books and materials to complete the activities:

Lessons From History (Elementary) by Dr. Jawanza Kunjufu (book and videotape)
Ashanti to Zulu by Margaret Musgrove
Colors Around Me by Vivian Church
Shining Legacy by Nkechi Taifa
Kwanzaa Coloring Book by Valerie Banks
Color Me Light of the World by Sharon N. Carter

There are other publications and audio-visuals that would be helpful but are not absolutely necessary. However, we hope you will utilize your resources (libraries, schools, videotape collection, friends, etc.) as well as continue to build your own library of African and African American History and Culture. There is one thing you must do before you go any further: Let your KUUMBA (Creativity) flow!!!

Correlation of SETCLAE Lessons to Academic Objectives

In an effort to accommodate the implementation of SETCLAE into the existing curriculum in your school, the HARAMBEE TIME sessions have been correlated to the most common academic objectives for this grade level. *The Typical Course of Study* for kindergarten through twelfth grade was compiled by World Book Educational Products. Curriculum materials such as *The Nault-Caswell-Brain Analysis of Courses of Study* and others from The National Council of Teachers of Mathematics, English, and Social Studies were analyzed in the preparation of the study guide. Please use this guide to help give SETCLAE a home in your setting. You will soon see that the program is a welcome and valuable member of the family and HARAMBEE TIME can be effective in "pulling us together" as we build Tomorrow's Leaders. We also encourage you to incorporate the learning and classroom management styles (e.g. student-made materials and Harambee Groups respectively) used in SETCLAE into all subjects taught. And share your success stories with your colleagues!

LA - Language Arts
SS - Social Studies
HT - Health
MT - Mathematics

1 - Let Me Introduce Myself
LA Penmanship
Completing sentences

2 - Bonding
LA Penmanship

3 - Rules, Rights, and Responsibilities
LA Deductive reasoning

4 - We Like That
LA Deductive reasoning
Penmanship

5 - Goal Setting
MT Counting to 100
LA Learning the Alphabet

6 - I Can Be!!!
Career Education
LA Using magazines

7 - Me and My Family
SS U.S. Geography
Our American culture
Our Native background

8 - Names We Call Ourselves
LA Completing sentences
SS Our American culture

9 - The Color Question
LA Creating stories
Word usage
Listening and speaking skills

10 - *Lessons* Video with Dr. Jawanza Kunjufu
LA Critique
SS Our American culture
HT Type and functions of food
Body's utilization of food

11 - Africa, The Continent
SS Map and globe skills
Our Native background
Exploration and Discovery

12 - Egypt is in Africa
SS Our Native background

13 - The African Triangle
SS Map and globe skills

14 - Freedom Fighters
LA Biographies of great Americans
SS U.S. Political System

15 - Sitting in the Front
LA Creative dramatics
Biographies of great Americans
SS U.S. Political System

16 - Lessons From History
SS African American History
Our American culture
LA Critical thinking skills

17 - African American Leaders
LA Using magazines
Biographies of great Americans

18 - Black Culture
LA Extended vocabulary
Word usage

19 - What Is Black English?
LA Speech
Language
Basic grammar

20 - Public Speaking
LA Listening and speaking activities

21 - Music...The Radio
LA Deductive reasoning
SS Contemporary music

22 - Time and How We Spend It
LA Deductive reasoning

23 - Television
LA Deductive reasoning
Completing sentences

24 - Values
LA Deductive reasoning

25 - Advertising Images
LA Using magazines
Critical thinking skills

26 - School!
LA Sentence writing skills

27 - Me and My Friends
LA Critical thinking skills

28 - How to Say No!
LA Critical thinking skills

29 - The Nguzo Saba - Seven Principles
LA Value Development
SS Our American culture

30 - Kuumba Means Creativity
SS Community empowerment

31 - Carla and Annie
LA Critical thinking skills

32 - Becoming a Man or Woman
SS Career selection

SETCLAE Vocabulary Means Word Power!!

You use words every day, when you talk to your family, friends, and teachers. New words are fun and easy to learn. By learning new words, you will become smart and be able to let everyone know what you think and how you feel.

Look at the words below and use them at home, school, and play.

Harambee Time #2
benefits

Harambee Time #3
discipline

Harambee Time #5
successful

Harambee Time #6
career

Harambee Time #8
ancestor
heritage

Harambee Time #10
skit

Harambee Time #11
Africa
pyramid

Harambee Time #12
Egypt

Harambee Time #13
continent

Harambee Time #14
Underground Railroad

Harambee Time #15
boycott

Harambee Time #18
culture

Harambee Time #23
commercial

Harambee Time #29
Nguzo Saba

The SETCLAE Student Profile (2nd Grade)

Name ____

Grade ____________________ Teacher ____________________________________

Date ____

Instructions

Please answer the following questions on the answer sheet and think very hard about how you really feel before answering each one. THERE ARE NO RIGHT or WRONG ANSWERS. We want YOUR answers. Your answers will help us teach you the kinds of lessons you would enjoy and benefit from the most during Harambee Time! Write all answers on the answer sheet ONLY!

Part I

Read each statement or question. If it is true for you, circle the answer YES on the answer sheet. If it is not true for you, circle the answer NO. Answer every question even if it's hard to decide. (Just think about yourself and what's important to you.) Circle only one answer for each question.

1. I like to be alone sometimes. a. Yes b. No
2. I like to stand in front of the class and speak. a. Yes b. No
3. When we are cleaning up our classroom, if I finish before everybody else, I play. a. Yes b. No
4. School will help me to be what I want to be. a. Yes b. No
5. If I can't think of anything good to say about someone, I don't say anything at all. a. Yes b. No
6. I know what kind of person I want to be when I grow up. a. Yes b. No
7. I like to play with my favorite toy all by myself more than I like to share it with others. a. Yes b. No
8. If things don't go my way, I get mad. a. Yes b. No
9. School is boring most of the time. a. Yes b. No
10. Do you speak slang? a. Yes b. No
11. If I don't see a trash can, I throw my trash on the ground. a. Yes b. No
12. In class, I like to raise my hand when the teacher wants somebody to do extra work. a. Yes b. No
13. Do you tell the truth most of the time? a. Yes b. No
14. Would you like to be in a family other than your own? a. Yes b. No

15. My neighborhood is a good place to live. a. Yes b. No
16. I like being with people that are different from me. a. Yes b. No
17. I like me! a. Yes b. No
18. I am happy whenever my friends have fun without me. a. Yes b. No
19. I like to hear bad things about someone and go tell somebody else. a. Yes b. No
20. When someone tells me that I did something wrong, I get mad. a. Yes b. No
21. When someone laughs at me, it bothers me. a. Yes b. No
22. When I talk to people, I look into their eyes. a. Yes b. No
23. If I had lots of money, I would be happy all the time. a. Yes b. No
24. When my schoolwork is good, it's because I tried very hard. a. Yes b. No
25. When my schoolwork is good, it's because I was lucky. a. Yes b. No
26. When I need help, I ask for it. a. Yes b. No
27. When the teacher leaves the room, I talk and get out of my seat. a. Yes b. No
28. I like TV because I learn a lot from it. a. Yes b. No

Part II

Read each item carefully. If it is something that is important to you, check the first box on the answer sheet. If it is not important to you (it doesn't really matter or have anything to do with you), check the second box. Take your time and think about it. There are no right or wrong answers. We want to know your feelings.

	Important to Me	Not Important to Me
1. Helping others	❑	❑
2. What others think of me	❑	❑
3. Reading	❑	❑
4. Television	❑	❑
5. Solving problems by fighting	❑	❑
6. Learning about my family members -- dead and living	❑	❑
7. Getting along with others	❑	❑
8. Doing whatever my friends do	❑	❑
9. Wearing expensive clothes	❑	❑
10. Doing well in school	❑	❑
11. Speaking up for myself and my ideas	❑	❑
12. Being positive most of the time	❑	❑
13. What it's like in Africa	❑	❑

Part III

Read each statement carefully. Read the choices. Then circle all the ones that best describe you and your feelings. Circle your answers on the answer sheet.

1. If asked to tell someone about myself, I would say things like:

   I'm fun to be around.
   I give up easily.
   I like helping others.
   I get bored a lot.
   I'm a leader.
   I like to get in trouble.
   I'm a good fighter.
   I'm happy.
   I'm slow.
   I'm unhappy.

2. If asked to tell somebody what I look like, I would say I am or have

   okay-looking
   skinny
   pretty eyes
   nice hair
   a head that is too big
   too short
   ugly
   light-skinned
   beautiful/handsome
   pretty skin
   too fat
   dark-skinned
   slim
   a nose that is too big

3. Circle one.

   I a. like my hair.
   b. don't like

4. I chose the above answer because my hair is:

   short
   curly
   light
   permed
   long
   nappy
   natural
   pressed
   thick
   dark
   braided
   straight
   red
   mine!

5. Circle one.

   I a. like my skin color.
   b. don't like

6. I chose the above answer because my skin is:

   dark light just right

7. Circle the five words that first come to your mind when you hear the word Africa.

   slavery
   far away
   Blacks
   kings and queens
   Tarzan
   jungle
   home
   ugly

8. Circle the one that is more important to you. Choose only one!

   a. being popular
   b. doing well in school

9. Answering these questions was

   a. great.
   b. hard.
   c. a good way to learn more about myself.
   d. silly.

Let Me Introduce Myself

Harambee Time #1

Materials:
- Pencil
- Index cards (1 per student)
- Arrange chairs in a circle (1 per student)

Procedure:
Be friendly! Introduce yourself to a classmate sitting near you and ask him or her the questions to the right.

Think of a word to describe someone with a letter that begins with the letter of his/her first name. For example:
Kind Keisha
Smiling Steven

Bring a photo of yourself to attach to your I.D. card.

NOTES:

____

____

____

____

____

____

____

✓ What is your favorite food?

____

✓ When is your birthday?

____

✓ What is your favorite TV show?

____

✓ What would you like to be when you grow up?

____

✓ What do you like most about yourself?

____

✓ Write two interesting things you learned about your classmate.

1. ______________________________________

2. ______________________________________

Use an index card to make your own I.D. card. It should look like this:

WHO AM I?

Name ______________________________

Address ______________________________

City, State, Zip ______________________________

Two Things I Like About Myself ______________________________

____

Something I Do Well ______________________________

____

____

Bonding

Harambee Time #2

MATERIALS:

- Glue
- Construction paper
- Coloring materials
- Scissors
- Personal photos brought from home

OPTIONAL MATERIALS:

- 5 sticks to attach to each group's flag
- *Ashanti to Zulu*

PROCEDURE:

Your teacher will help you and your classmates form Harambee Groups. Harambee means "Let's pull together". Pick a name from one of the five groups listed.

To learn more about groups 2, 3, and 4, read the section "SOMETHING YOU SHOULD KNOW".

What are the names of some other groups that work well together?

LIST SOME BENEFITS OF WORKING IN THESE GROUP ACTIVITIES: STUDYING SINGING IN A YOUTH CHOIR, SCOUTING, AND BEING ON A SWIM TEAM.

GROUP 1	GROUP 2	GROUP 3	GROUP 4	GROUP 5
Lions	Nigeria	Ashanti	Morehouse College	Scientists
Tigers	Kenya	Pondo	Hampton University	Lawyers
Bears	Egypt	Fanti	Spelman College	Artists
Giraffes	Azania	Ikoma	Tuskegee Institute	Teachers
Zebras	Tanzania	Chagga	Howard University	Farmers

Glue your photo onto your I.D. card. Your Harambee Group should make a group flag. Write your group's name on the flag along with the name of each group member. Use big letters. Make sure you decorate both sides of the flag. Introduce your group to the class and tell why the group chose its particular name. At the end of this Harambee, place your I.D. card in the "Tomorrow's Leaders" container.

MATERIALS:
- Chalkboard or flipchart
- Plan to sit in a circle

PROCEDURE:
Listed are rules. Some of the rules only apply to school. Others are only used at home or when playing. Rules should be used at school and home/play. Circle S if the rule is only for school, H if the rule is only for home or play and B if the rule should be used in both places.

NOTES:

Rules, Rights, and Responsibilities

Harambee Time #3

Today we are going to make rules for the classroom.

Discipline means self-control.

Why do we have rules?

What is a right?

What is a responsibility?

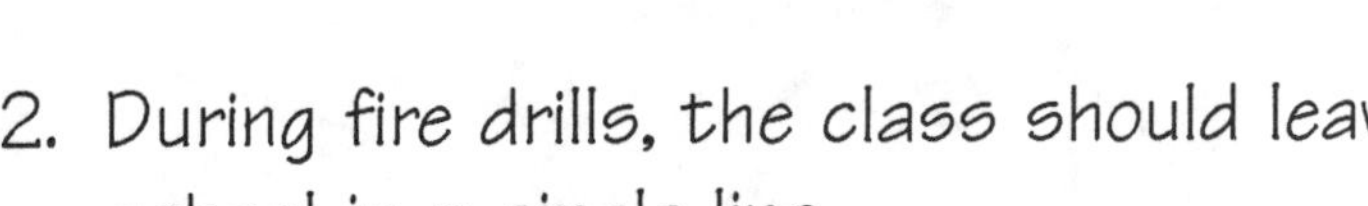

1. No fighting is allowed.	S	H	B
2. During fire drills, the class should leave school in a single line.	S	H	B
3. I must not take anyone's property without asking.	S	H	B
4. When the teacher leaves the room, I must remain in my seat.	S	H	B
5. I must make my bed everyday.	S	H	B

MATERIALS: (HG)

- Paper cut into strips long enough for 5-10 phrases to be pasted onto large poster board
- Coloring materials
- Box/container for MZURI Box
- Construction paper
- Glue

PROCEDURE:

Each member of your Harambee Group should think of a good deed a classmate has done. Write this good deed on a strip of paper. All strips of paper will be used to make a BIG poster. Glue the strips on a poster board and decorate it.

NOTES:

____

____

____

____

____

____

____

____

____

____

____

We Like That!

Harambee Time #4

Sometimes people do things that make you feel good, such as: Helping you clean up or working quietly when you don't feel well.

Sometimes people do things that make you feel sad: Taking your pencil without asking or making a lot of noise when you're trying to work. When someone does something that we like; we're going to say a chant. The chant is: "WE LIKE THAT ... AND THAT'S THE WAY IT IS!"

You can also help make an MZURI (Good) box. Decorate the box using construction paper, coloring materials and glue. When a student does something nice, his/her name and the good deed will be written on a card, then placed in a box. When the teacher pulls his/her name, that person will receive a special treat.

How do you feel when someone says something nice about you?

How do you feel when you say something nice about someone?

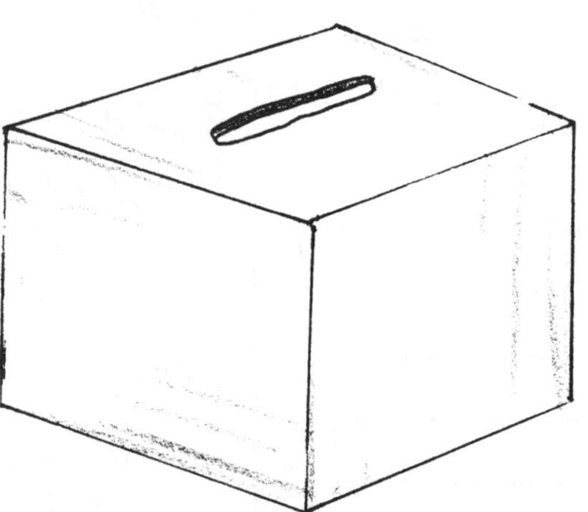

Goal Setting

Harambee Time #5

MATERIALS:

✏ paper

PROCEDURE:

In order to be successful, you must have goals that you try to achieve.
Let's think of some goals and practice them.

Perhaps you might like to try:

✔ subtracting in your head

✔ drawing a picture of yourself

✔ spelling a word that begins with each letter of the alphabet

NOTES:

I WANT TO. . . SO I WILL. . .

Write your goal here and begin practicing how to achieve it.

Draw a picture inside each box of you working toward your goal.

1.	2.
3.	4.

MATERIALS:
- 26 Index cards
- Outstanding Black Americans posters
- Write the alphabet on the board with space between each letter

PROCEDURE:
Answer the following:
What is a career?

What are some of the careers that people in your family have?

Let's see how many other careers we can think of. The more careers you can think of, the more you can do.

✔ To discuss:
What kind of work is involved in different careers?

What kind of training is needed?

In what kind of setting is the work done?

Who are some of the people in the field and how can you meet them?

I Can Be...!

Harambee Time #6

Use the posters to complete the spelling of a career you might choose someday.

1. w r ___ ___ ___ ___
2. ___ a ___ ___ e ___
3. m ___ ___ ___ c ___ ___ n
4. ___ ___ i ___ n t ___ ___ ___
5. a ___ h ___ e ___ ___
6. ___ e ___ c ___ ___ r

Homework:
Have your family help you learn more about a career of interest to you. Share what you learned with the class.

MATERIALS:

- Picture of families
- *Lessons From History*, p. 100
- Paper
- *Kwanzaa*, p. 32-37
- *Ashanti to Zulu*

PROCEDURE:

Think about it:
What is a family?

How many in your family live with you?

What member of your family do you spend the most time with?

What does your family like to do together?

Collect pictures of your family and make a personal photo album.

NOTES:

____

____

____

____

____

____

____

Me and My Family

Harambee Time #7

Talk to older members of your family (grandparents, great grandparents, aunts, uncles, or cousins). They have years of wisdom and experience. They are living libraries and remember events you read about today. Talk with them and ask questions. Write some questions you would like to ask an older member of your family.

1. ____

2. ____

3. ____

4. ____

5. ____

6. ____

Names We Call Ourselves

Harambee Time #8

MATERIALS:

- *Color Me Light of the World*, p. 11
- *Lessons From History*, preface
- Paper
- Coloring materials
- Globe or map

PROCEDURE:

Things to Consider:
Look at the picture in *Color Me Light of the World.*
Describe what you see.

What is different about each child?

What is an ancestor?

Where did their ancestors live?

Where did your ancestors come from?

What is your heritage?

What is an ethnic group?

Why are black people most accurately called African Americans?

NOTES:

____

____

____

Tell a story about your heritage, your present and what you would like to see happen in your future.

- ✔ Draw a picture of yourself. The way you look is part of your heritage.
- ✔ Choose a name for yourself that reflects your heritage.
- ✔ Create a poem describing yourself using the following format:

I am ____ .

I have ____ .

(2 words describing your appearance)

I like ____________________ , ____________________ , and

(3 action words/verbs)

____________________ .

I am ____ .

(2 positive words to describe your personality)

and I can ____ .

(something you do well).

The Color Question

Harambee Time #9

MATERIALS:
- *Colors Around Me*
- Paper
- Coloring materials

PROCEDURE:
Something to think about:

Why are we different colors?

What are some of the benefits of having dark skin?

Does the color of a person's skin make him/her a mean person?

Have you ever been teased because of your skin color?

Do you call other children names because of their color?

NOTES:

____

____

____

____

____

African Americans come in many beautiful shades. Listed below are some words that describe some of these shades. Use the letters in parentheses to make the words complete.

1. __ h __ c o l __ t e (c, o, a)
2. c o __ f e __ (f, e)
3. l i c o __ __ c __ (r, i, e)
4. p __ __ c h (e, a)
5. c i n __ a __ o __ (n, n, m)
6. __ o __ p e r (c, p)
7. __ a n (t)
8. b r __ __ n (o, w)

MATERIALS: (HG)
- *Lessons* Video
- Television and Video Recorder

PROCEDURE:
Something to consider:

What lessons did you learn from the video?

Who were those people named in the chants?

What word are we never going to use again?

With your Harambee Group, create a short skit based on what you learned from this video. Write about the characters (names of persons who will be in the skit), the setting (area where the story takes place) and the props (objects used in the story-like tables and chairs).

NOTES:

Lessons Video with Dr. Jawanza Kunjufu

Harambee Time #10

Write your play here.

What lessons can you share with a family member or friend?

Africa, The Continent

Harambee Time #11

MATERIALS:
- ✏ *Lessons From History*, Chap. 1 (1 each)
- ✏ Coloring materials
- ✏ Dictionary
- ✏ *Color Me Light*, p. 19 (1 each)
- ✏ *Ashanti to Zulu*

PROCEDURE:
From *Lessons From History*, please answer the following: What is the most interesting thing you learned about Africa?

✔ Using your dictionary, look up the words in *Lessons From History* that you do not understand.

✔ Complete the following: "It's nice to know that Africa. . ."

✔ Write three sentences using some of the new words you learned that taught you something new about Africa.

What is the weather like in most of Africa? (p. 1)

Is Africa a country or continent? (p. 2)

Where were the great pyramids built? (p. 2-3)

What do you think it was like to live in Africa a long time ago? (p. 5)

In Africa, what is the sign of life? (p. 6)

Who can name an African country? (p. 7)

What are some of the things that made Africa a very rich land? (p. 9)

Does this look like any place you have ever been? (p. 10)

Egypt is in Africa

Harambee Time #12

MATERIALS:
- *Lessons From History*, p. 2-4, 7, and 47
- Crayons
- Map of Africa or world globe
- Pictures of Egypt

PROCEDURE:
Write two complete sentences on what you've learned about Africa and Egypt. On a separate sheet of paper, draw something you would see in Egypt. Use the "code key" to discover an important message.

CODE KEY

10=A	13=B
1=C	5=D
9=E	11=F
3=G	7=H
8=I	25=J
6=K	15=L
14=M	4=N
2=O	26=P
9=Q	17=R
20=S	24=T
23=U	18=V
22=W	16=X
21=Y	12=Z

Review the pages from *Lessons* to fill in the blanks.

1. There are many ______________ in Egypt. (p. 2)
2. ______________________________ drew the plans for the first pyramid. (p. 2)
3. Imhotep was the father of ______________________________ (p. 3)
4. Africans founded the first ______________ (p. 4)
5. __________________ was King of Egypt. (p. 47)

In the space below, draw something you would see in Egypt.

___ ___ ___ ___ ___
9 3 21 26 24

___ ___
8 20

___ ___
8 4

___ ___ ___ ___ ___ ___
10 11 17 8 1 10!

The African Triangle

Harambee Time #13

MATERIALS:(HG)

- *Lessons From History*, p. 22, 81
- *The Great Encounter*, p. 11-16
- World map and/or globe
- Magazines (*Ebony, Essence, Black Enterprise, National Geographic*)
- Scissors

PROCEDURE:

With your Harambee Group, discuss the following: In which state do you live? What country?
Who has travelled to other parts of the USA?
Where? What was it like?
Was it the same/different as home?
Has anybody been to places outside of the USA?
What was it like?
Were the people different or did some of them look like you (us)?
What is an island?

After your teacher reads pages from *The Great Encounter*, answer these questions:

1. Ade' and his father were from which continent in the African Triangle? ______________________
2. Which continent were they travelling to that was also part of the African Triangle? ______________________
3. Did Africans come to America before Columbus? ____________

MATERIALS: (HG)

- *Shining Legacy*, p. 18-20
- *Lessons From History*, p. 24-26
- Outstanding Black American posters

PROCEDURE:

Why was learning to read so important?

Do you like to read?

Did Africans like being slaves?

What did they do that shows they did not like being slaves?
What would you have done?

✔ Form Harambee Groups and learn one verse from the poem.

NOTES:

____

____

____

____

____

____

____

____

____

Freedom Fighters

Harambee Time #14

Harriet was strong, she never
went wrong.
Listen to the legend of Harriet
Tubman
For you will see what strength
is all about
That she was a warrior in every
sense of the word
There is definitely no doubt
Born in Maryland on the
Eastern Shore
A strong field slave was she
She worked so hard 'til her
bones were sore
But she always yearned to
be free
One night Harriet said she could take this no more
And decided it was time to escape
She fled through fields and farms, past plantations and barns
'til she reached North where she could stay
But while "free" in the North, she had few friends
For they were all still in the South
So she worked very hard and with the money she saved
She went back South to free HUNDREDS OF SLAVES
WHAT WAS THIS UNDERGROUND RAILROAD?
WAS IT A REAL TRAIN WITH TRACKS?
oh no, but the Underground Railroad
Was a secret escape system for Blacks
She could not read, nor could she write
BUT THOUSANDS OF TIMES, SHE OUTWITTED THE WHITES
Like Nzinga before, and Assata after.
HARRIET WAS STRONG, SHE NEVER WENT WRONG
HARRIET WAS STRONG, SHE NEVER WENT WRONG!
Excerpts from "Harriet Was Strong: She Never Went Wrong"

(From *Shining Legacy* by Nkechi Taifa, 1983, Washington, D.C., House of Songhay)

Sitting in the Front

Harambee Time #15

MATERIALS:

- *Lessons From History*, p. 39-41
- Pictures of Rosa Parks and the Montgomery bus boycotts
- Construction paper
- Coloring materials

PROCEDURE:

Something to discuss: When you can sit wherever you want, where do you sit? Why?

Why is it good to sit in the front of the class?

What is a boycott?

Why was there a bus boycott in Montgomery?

Could African Americans eat in any restaurant they wanted?

Use construction paper and coloring materials to make a sign that says: "I CAN SIT WHERE I LIKE!"

Write the correct word for each definition.

restaurant	boycott	bus	laws	Rosa Parks

1. ____________________ a large vehicle to ride in with other passengers
2. ____________________ expressing protest by not spending money in a particular place
3. ____________________ a public eating place
4. ____________________ a brave woman who was arrested for sitting where she pleased
5. ____________________ a set of rules to follow

MATERIALS:
✏ Paper

PROCEDURE:
Something to discuss:

- ✔ What is history?
- ✔ How important is history to us?
- ✔ What are some of the lessons we can learn?
- ✔ Should you follow rules? Why?
- ✔ Is it bad to lie?
- ✔ Do you have to fight for freedom?
- ✔ Have others?
- ✔ How did African American people survive slavery?

NOTES:

____

____

____

____

____

____

____

____

Lessons From History

Harambee Time #16

Fill in the blanks using the following words:

mistakes	felt	teach	great
past	history	lived	

I like to study the past. It's called ________. When I learn about the ________, I can see where ________ were made and learn how people ________ and ________ about things. When I grow up, I will ________ my history to others so they too may know how ________ our ancestors were and how much we can do.

MATERIALS:

- *Outstanding Black American posters*
- *Great Negroes*

PROCEDURE:

Your class should review and discuss the African American leaders on the posters. Then you should complete the exercise by drawing a line from the leader's name to the letter in front of his/her accomplishment.

You will be a leader someday. What great things would you like to do to help your people?

NOTES:

____

____

____

____

____

____

____

____

____

____

____

____

African American Leaders

Harambee Time #17

1. Charles Drew
2. Lorraine Hansberry
3. Booker T. Washington
4. Jesse Jackson
5. Bill Cosby
6. Marian Anderson
7. Wilma Rudolph
8. Malcolm X
9. Percy L. Julian
10. Harriet Tubman

A. An Olympic gold medalist

B. Gave millions to Black colleges

C. World-famous opera singer

D. Freed hundreds of slaves

E. Muslim minister, human rights leader

F. Pioneer in plasma research

G. Famous scientist

H. Wrote "Raisin in the Sun"

I. Ran for President in 1984 and 1988

J. Founded Tuskegee Institute

When you have learned more about these excellent leaders, pretend you're a radio or TV news reporter about to conduct an interview for a story. Pick one leader to interview and write your interview questions on a separate sheet of paper. Read *Great Negroes* for more information.

Black Culture

Harambee Time #18

MATERIALS: (HG)
- *Lessons From History*, p. 73-88
- Red, black, and green crayons
- Cut-out of Africa for tracing, (p. 1 in *Lessons*)
- *Colors Around Me*
- *Kwanzaa Coloring Book*
- Musical selections from African American culture

PROCEDURE:
All people have a culture, including African Americans. Use the pages from *Lessons From History* (look in parentheses) to fill in the blanks:

Our culture is.....
what we eat: mangos, avocados, and blackeye __________ (p. 84)
what we wear: a dashiki, a gele, and kente __________ (p. 82)
what we sing: gospel, blues, reggae and jazz __________ (p. 85)
what we speak: (clue: It's an African language) __________ (p. 79)
what we believe: "My concern is for__________" (p. 73)

Each Harambee Group should choose one of the 5 activities listed below and present the project to the class:

1. Sing the first verse of "Lift Every Voice and Sing".

2. Make the Liberation flag (read pp. 76-77 in *Lessons*) and who created it and what each color stands for.

3. Write and read a poem about what you've learned about Black culture.

4. Make a large, colorful poster that shows examples of Black culture. Include food, clothing, musical instruments. Be able to identify the items that are in the poster.

5. Write and sing a rap on what you know about Black culture.

MATERIALS: (HG)
✏ *Cornrows*

What Is Black English?

Harambee Time #19

PROCEDURE:
Consider the following:
What is Black English?

What is a dialect?

What is Standard English?

What is bilingual?

Is Black English acceptable? When? Where?

Is it important to be able to speak Standard English?

Each Harambee Group is given 4 sentences. Working together, they should decide if the sentence is using Black English or Standard English. The teacher will ask each group for their response as he/she goes through the questions.

GROUP #1

1. He be goin' to work lookin' dirty every day.
2. I have to go to the store later.
3. He don't look good in that shirt.
4. We have to start heading home at 4:00.

GROUP #2

5. I asked Jomo to come.
6. I don't have any more candy.
7. I'm going downtown later.
8. I gotta go home at 4:00.

GROUP #3

9. I ast' Jomo do he wanna come.
10. I ain't got no mo candy.
11. I'm fixin' to go downtown.
12. Tanisha went to Stephanie's house.

GROUP #4

13. I'm going to the park when I finish my homework.
14. Tanisha over Stephanie house.
15. I'mma go to the park when I get through with my homework.
16. I got me some dollars.

GROUP #5

17. What time is it?
18. Don't be messin' with me.
19. Please leave me alone!
20. I'mma go to the store.

Public Speaking

Harambee Time #20

MATERIALS:

- Paper
- A different number on a strip of paper (1 each)

PROCEDURE:

How useful is good public speaking?

✔ Practice these qualities of a good public speaker. Use them when you speak. Look at the people listening to you. Speak loud. Stand straight and tall. Talk about something you like.

Who are some people you like to hear?

Why are they great speakers?

NOTES:

When your number is called, go to the front of the class and talk about one of these subjects: what you like about school, your favorite family vacation, or what you like to do at home.

Draw a picture of yourself as a great speaker.

MATERIALS: (HG)

- FM radio
- Recording of a popular song

Music...The Radio

Harambee Time #21

PROCEDURE:

Each member is to write two sentences. One sentence should be about him or herself. The other sentence should deal with what they like about their group. All groups will present their song to the class. Call it "THE HARAMBEE SONG".

What is your song's message?

Listen to the recording. What's the first thing you notice about a song? (Circle One):

The Music

The Words

NOTES:

____

____

____

____

____

____

____

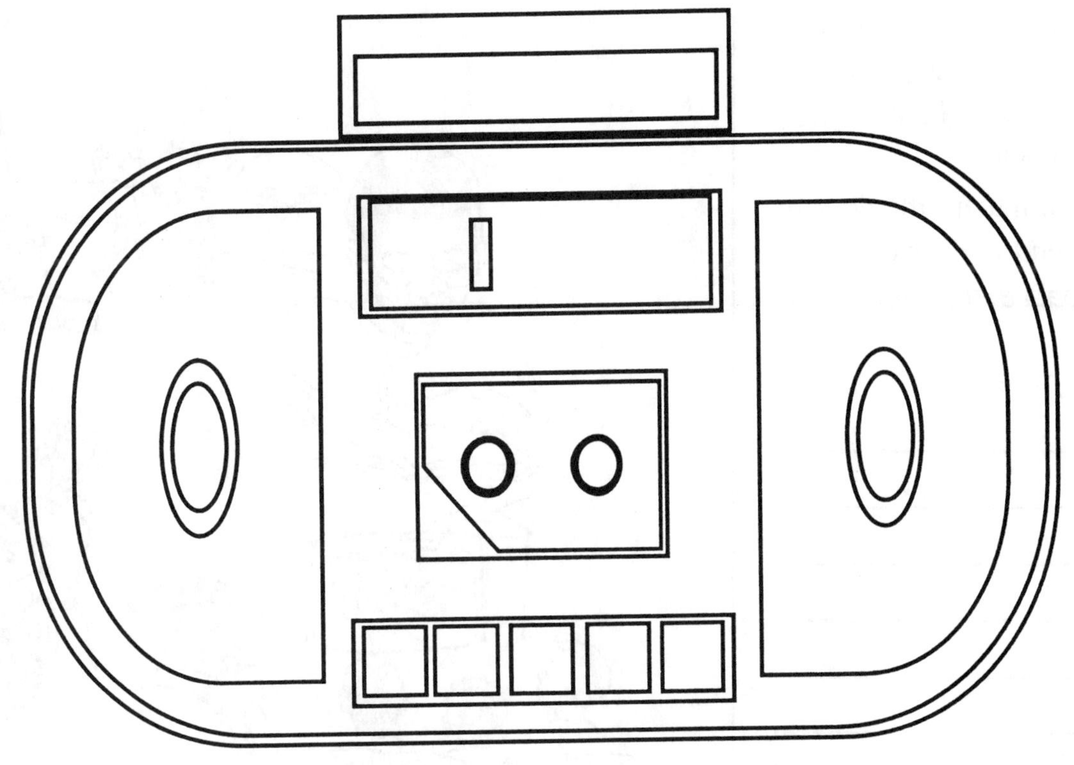

MATERIALS:
- Children's books
- Visible clocks
- Sand clock
- Crayons

Time and How We Spend It

Harambee Time #22

PROCEDURE:
How many hours are you in school each day?
How many hours do you watch TV at home?
How many hours do you spend outside, playing?
How much time do you spend with your family?
What do you spend time doing?
How many minutes is your favorite TV show?
How many hours do you read or do homework?
What is your goal?
What are you doing to reach it?
How much time do you spend working on your goals every day?

NOTES:

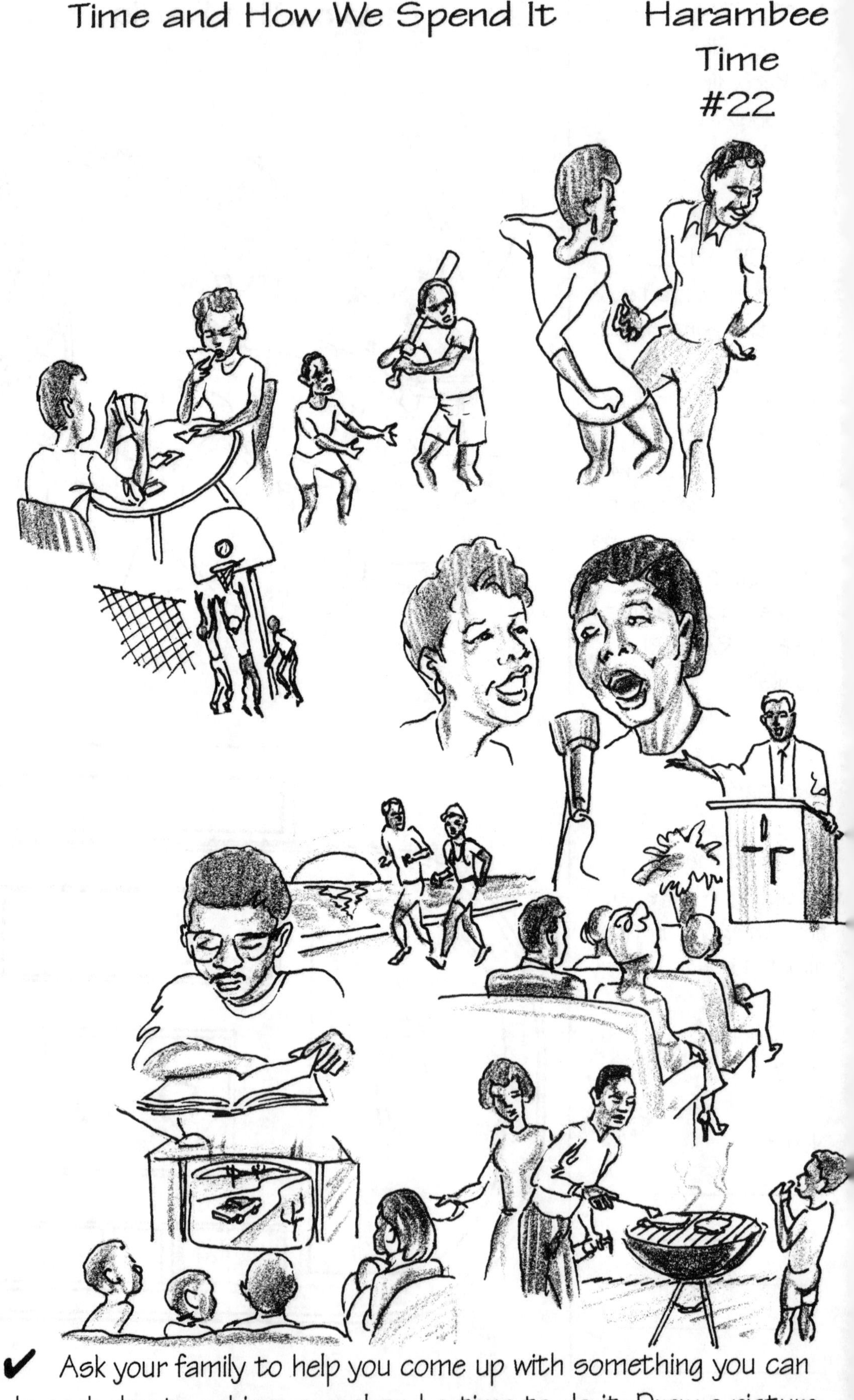

✔ Ask your family to help you come up with something you can do each day to achieve a goal and a time to do it. Draw a picture of what you like to spend time doing, when you're at home.

MATERIALS:
- TV
- Pen
- Paper

Television

Harambee Time #23

PROCEDURE:

How much time do you spend watching TV every day?

What is your favorite TV show?

What do you like about the program?

Does the rest of your family like your favorites?

What is your favorite commercial?

What do you like about it?

When you go to the store, do you ask your parent(s) to buy the product in the commercials you see on TV?

What do you think you learn from your favorite TV show?

Are these things good or bad?

Television shows are not all the same. Some shows fit in different groups like the ones listed below:

NEWS:
A program that tells you what happens in the world (What adults watch late at night or early in the morning).

COMEDY:
A show that makes you laugh (The Fresh Prince of Bel Air).

DRAMA:
A show that is serious (Star Trek).

Choose a show to watch and write a report to share with your class. Write this information (Ask a parent or other family member to help you):

Name of the show:
What day of the week is it on?
What time does the show come on? ____ am or ____ pm
(Note: am is for morning time, pm is for evening time)
What are some good things about this show?
What are some bad things about this show?
How would you make it better?
Is it news, comedy or drama? (Your show may not belong in any of these groups, but that's okay)

MATERIALS:
- A mirror (represents student)
- A 1-dollar bill (represents money)
- *Sparkle*, p. 5 (represents friends)
- *Carla and Annie*, p. 8 (represents family)
- Chairs in a semi-circle facing board and props

PROCEDURE:
Look at the dollar bill your teacher has. As the teacher reads from *Sparkle* and *Carla and Annie* think about the following:
What does important mean?

What things are most important to you?

What would you like to do more than anything else in the world?
Is it something to do with your friends? family? money? or self?

What do you own that is more important to you than anything else?

What is the one thing you would like to own more than anything else?

Did you think that money was the most important thing?

Values

Harambee Time #24

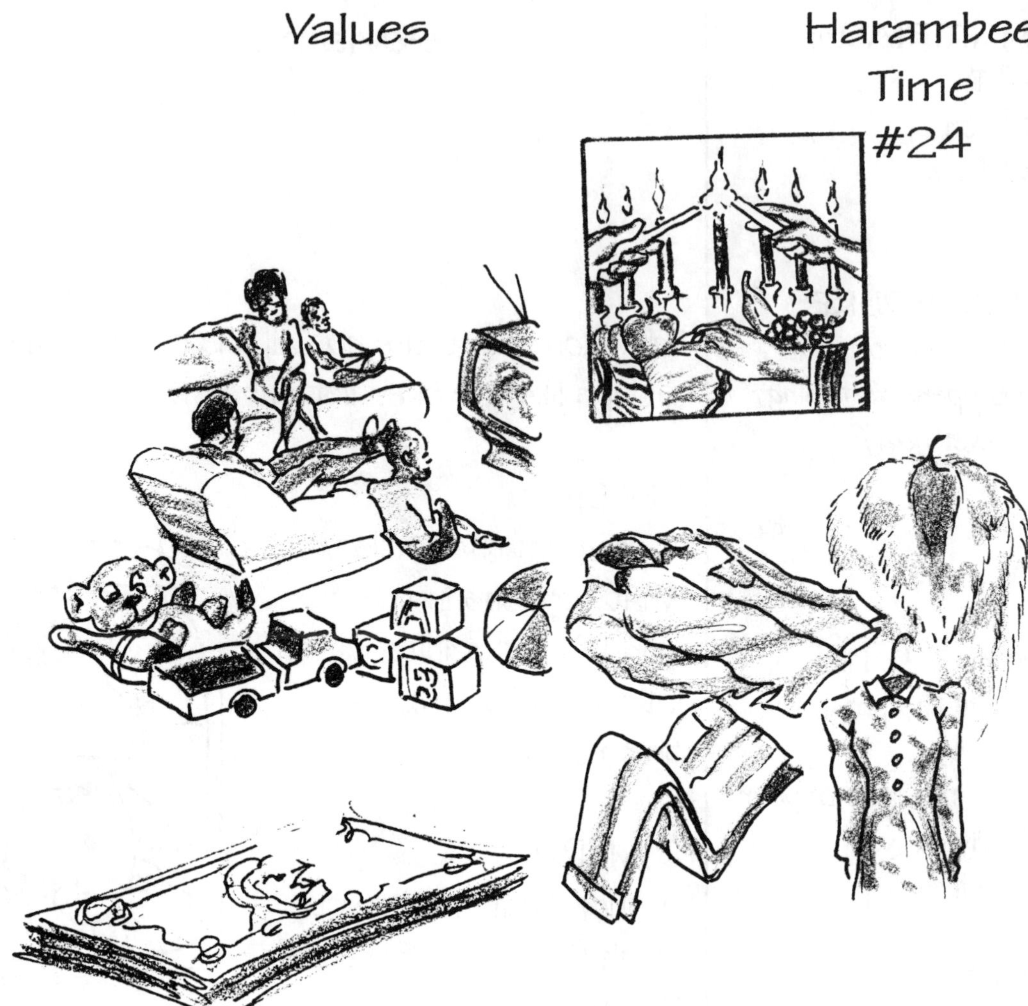

Choose the correct word for each sentence.

share kind money love respect

1. Sparkle learned to ________ her things.
2. All people should be ________ to each other.
3. You need ________ to buy things at a store.
4. I ________ my parents.
5. We must ________ our teacher and classroom rules.

Which of these four items will help you the most in being a better person?
Circle one: money family friends clothes

Why did you choose this answer?

Advertising Images

Harambee Time #25

MATERIALS:

- Pencil
- Popular magazines (*Ebony, Essence,* entertainment, fashion)
- Scissors
- Coloring materials
- Paper

PROCEDURE:

Do you know what advertisements are?

What is your favorite commercial?

Why do you like it?

What are they trying to get you to buy?

Does the commercial make you want to buy it? Why? Why not?

NOTES:

There are many kinds of products being advertised in magazines. You will see cars, food, make-up, hair products and other items. Cut out an ad that you really like and answer the following questions:

1. Why did you choose this ad?
2. What is the product?
3. Do you think it costs a lot of money or very little?
4. Is there a pretty woman or handsome man in the ad?

Use this ad to make your own ad. Draw a product on a separate sheet of paper. Name it and write under the picture the type of product it is.

Why should someone buy your product. What will it do for them?

School!

Harambee Time #26

MATERIALS: (HG)

- *Sparkle*, p. 4-7
  I'm Special, Too, p. 21
- Paper
- Pencil
- Pictures of educational settings

PROCEDURE:

After your teacher reads from *Sparkle* and *I'm Special, Too* answer these questions:

Why do we come to school?

Do you think schools do what they are supposed to do?

How could they be better?

What people make up all the parts of school?

NOTES:

____

____

____

____

____

____

____

____

____

____

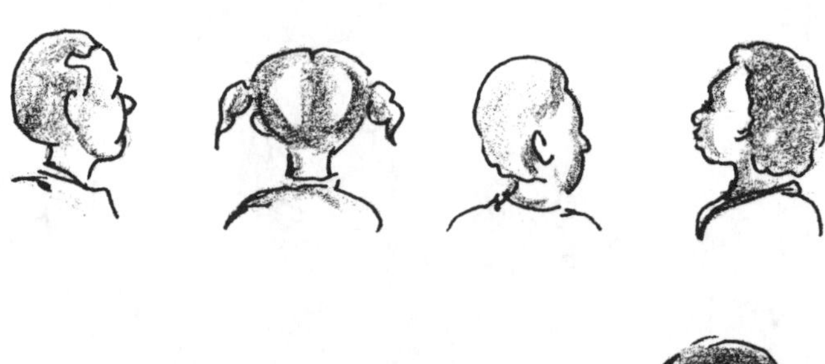

Because you are now a 2nd grader, you can share what you have learned with children younger than yourself. Say this rhyme: "Each one, teach one." This means each of you will teach someone else what you have learned. Working with your Harambee Group, make a lesson sheet for younger grades. Keep it simple. Some suggestions are writing numbers 1 to 20, colors, or the alphabet. Ask your teacher for help.

MATERIALS:
- *Sparkle*, pp. 1-5
- Coloring materials

PROCEDURE:
Discuss the following:
Why do you think Sparkle was friends with Marsha?

Why is it no one would be friends with Marsha?

Did her clothes/ appearance make her a mean or bad person?

Who is your friend and why?

What do you like about your friends?

Do you ever get angry with them?

What do you do when you become angry?

How do you help your friends? How do your friends help you?

NOTES:

____

____

____

____

Me and My Friends

Harambee Time #27

Draw a picture of you and your friend having fun together. What's the best thing about having friends?

MATERIALS:
✏ Paper

PROCEDURE:
How do you choose your friends?

Would a true friend try to force you into doing something bad?

NOTES:

How to Say No

Harambee Time #28

Read the examples listed:

A student is asked to take the attendance sheet to the office. S/he sees a friend in the hallway who tries to get him/her to go into the bathroom and play with a water gun. What should S/he do?

A neighbor who knows you cannot have company when your mother is not home insists on coming inside your house to play with your Nintendo. What do you do?

A friend offers you some candy that s/he stole from the corner store. What do you do?

Three of your friends are calling you a nerd because you want to finish your homework before coming outside to play. They didn't even bring their books home. What do you do?

Some friends insist that you will not get hurt if you use an electric saw to cut some wood. What do you do?

Some people will tell you to do something wrong or bad just to get you in trouble. A true friend won't do this. If anyone tells you to steal, cheat, disobey rules, take drugs or anything else wrong, what should you do?

MATERIALS:(HG)
✏ *Lessons From History*, p. 74

The Nguzo Saba (Seven Principles)

Harambee Time #29

PROCEDURE:
The word principle means "rule".
Rules are made for our own good.
There are rules for safety, to keep order and rules to help us, our families and communities.
Nguzo Saba is Kiswahili for seven principles.

Discuss the principles and how you can practice them everyday.

NOTES:

UMOJA - Everyone should be nice when working and playing together.

KUJICHAGULIA - When trying to do something good, don't give up.

UJIMA - Help other people.

UJAMAA - Share with others.

NIA - Make your group the best it can be.

KUUMBA - Help keep your school and home clean.

IMANI - Believe in your family, teachers, and leaders.

Unscramble these Kiswahili words and write the definition:

GZOUN BASA

Definition: ______________________________

Each Harambee Group is to choose one of the seven principles and put together a skit that will show the class how each principle is used.

MATERIALS:

- *Lessons From History*, p. 74
- Crayons
- Gloves and garbage cans

PROCEDURE:

Why is our community dirty in some areas?

Who litters in our community?

How can we use Kuumba to improve our community?

Draw other items that help adults and children keep their community clean.

NOTES:

____

____

____

____

____

____

____

____

____

____

____

____

Kuumba Means Creativity

Harambee Time #30

Repeat the following:

Kuumba - Creativity. To do always as much as we can in the way we can, in order to leave our community more beautiful than we inherited it.

During recess or after school, your class should use gloves and garbage cans to clean up the area around your school. Ask the janitor or custodian to help you.

MATERIALS:
- *Carla and Annie*, p. 11-15
- Pencil

PROCEDURE:
Consider the following: Describe the feelings of the characters in *Carla and Annie* in various scenes. How did Carla help Annie feel good about herself?

1. What did Annie's mother tell her daughter about Carla?

2. How did this make Carla feel?

3. How would you feel?

4. Who helped Carla feel better about herself?

5. How did this person help Carla feel better?

6. Do you know anyone like Annie?

7. Should you be hurt or angry with them? Why or why not?

8. How can you help him or her?

Carla and Annie

Harambee Time #31

List some of the benefits of having darker skin. People of all races can be friends! Draw a picture of yourself and a friend from another race.

MATERIALS:
✏ Art paper and crayons

PROCEDURE:
Think about it:
When do you become a man or woman?

What do men and women do?

Will you look different?

Close your eyes and imagine you are a man or woman. Draw a picture of how you would like to look as an adult. What famous African American man or woman do you admire enough to want to imitate?

NOTES:

____

____

____

____

____

____

____

____

____

____

____

Becoming a Man or Woman

Harambee Time #32

Children go through different stages as they become adults. A few years from now, you will be a teenager. You will be taller and heavier. Your body will change. You will be one step closer to being an adult. There are some things only men can do, some things only women can do, and some things both can do. Listed below are some things adults do. Circle W if only women can do it, M if only men can do it and B if both can do it.

1. Cry	W	M	B
2. Cook and clean house	W	M	B
3. Have babies	W	M	B
4. Drive a car	W	M	B
5. Develop hips and breasts	W	M	B
6. Become president of United States	W	M	B
7. Go to work	W	M	B
8. Play professional football	W	M	B
9. Grow a beard	W	M	B

The SETCLAE Student Profile (2nd Grade)

Name ______________________________

Grade ______________ Teacher ______________________

Date ______________________________

Instructions

Please answer the following questions on the answer sheet and think very hard about how you really feel before answering each one. THERE ARE NO RIGHT or WRONG ANSWERS. We want YOUR answers. Your answers will help us teach you the kinds of lessons you would enjoy and benefit from the most during Harambee Time! Write all answers on the answer sheet ONLY!

Part I

Read each statement or question. If it is true for you, circle the answer YES on the answer sheet. If it is not true for you, circle the answer NO. Answer every question even if it's hard to decide. (Just think about yourself and what's important to you.) Circle only one answer for each question.

1. I like to be alone sometimes. a. Yes b. No
2. I like to stand in front of the class and speak. a. Yes b. No
3. When we are cleaning up our classroom, if I finish before everybody else, I play. a. Yes b. No
4. School will help me to be what I want to be. a. Yes b. No
5. If I can't think of anything good to say about someone, I don't say anything at all. a. Yes b. No
6. I know what kind of person I want to be when I grow up. a. Yes b. No
7. I like to play with my favorite toy all by myself more than I like to share it with others. a. Yes b. No
8. If things don't go my way, I get mad. a. Yes b. No
9. School is boring most of the time. a. Yes b. No
10. Do you speak slang? a. Yes b. No
11. If I don't see a trash can, I throw my trash on the ground. a. Yes b. No
12. In class, I like to raise my hand when the teacher wants somebody to do extra work. a. Yes b. No
13. Do you tell the truth most of the time? a. Yes b. No
14. Would you like to be in a family other than your own? a. Yes b. No

15. My neighborhood is a good place to live. a. Yes b. No
16. I like being with people that are different from me. a. Yes b. No
17. I like me! a. Yes b. No
18. I am happy whenever my friends have fun without me. a. Yes b. No
19. I like to hear bad things about someone and go tell somebody else. a. Yes b. No
20. When someone tells me that I did something wrong, I get mad. a. Yes b. No
21. When someone laughs at me, it bothers me. a. Yes b. No
22. When I talk to people, I look into their eyes. a. Yes b. No
23. If I had lots of money, I would be happy all the time. a. Yes b. No
24. When my schoolwork is good, it's because I tried very hard. a. Yes b. No
25. When my schoolwork is good, it's because I was lucky. a. Yes b. No
26. When I need help, I ask for it. a. Yes b. No
27. When the teacher leaves the room, I talk and get out of my seat. a. Yes b. No
28. I like TV because I learn a lot from it. a. Yes b. No

Part II

Read each item carefully. If it is something that is important to you, check the first box on the answer sheet. If it is not important to you (it doesn't really matter or have anything to do with you), check the second box. Take your time and think about it. There are no right or wrong answers. We want to know your feelings.

	Important to Me	Not Important to Me
1. Helping others	❑	❑
2. What others think of me	❑	❑
3. Reading	❑	❑
4. Television	❑	❑
5. Solving problems by fighting	❑	❑
6. Learning about my family members -- dead and living	❑	❑
7. Getting along with others	❑	❑
8. Doing whatever my friends do	❑	❑
9. Wearing expensive clothes	❑	❑
10. Doing well in school	❑	❑
11. Speaking up for myself and my ideas	❑	❑
12. Being positive most of the time	❑	❑
13. What it's like in Africa	❑	❑

Part III

Read each statement carefully. Read the choices. Then circle all the ones that best describe you and your feelings. Circle your answers on the answer sheet.

1. If asked to tell someone about myself, I would say things like:

I'm fun to be around.	I'm a leader.	I'm happy.
I give up easily.	I like to get in trouble.	I'm slow.
I like helping others.	I'm a good fighter.	I'm unhappy.
I get bored a lot.		

2. If asked to tell somebody what I look like, I would say I am or have

okay-looking	too short	too fat
skinny	ugly	dark-skinned
pretty eyes	light-skinned	slim
nice hair	beautiful/handsome	a nose that is too big
a head that is too big	pretty skin	

3. Circle one.
   I a. like my hair.
   b. don't like

4. I chose the above answer because my hair is:

short	permed	natural	dark	red
curly	long	pressed	braided	mine!
light	nappy	thick	straight	

5. Circle one.
   I a. like my skin color.
   b. don't like

6. I chose the above answer because my skin is:
   dark light just right

7. Circle the five words that first come to your mind when you hear the word Africa.

slavery	Tarzan
far away	jungle
Blacks	home
kings and queens	ugly

8. Circle the one that is more important to you. Choose only one!
   a. being popular
   b. doing well in school

9. Answering these questions was
   a. great.
   b. hard.
   c. a good way to learn more about myself.
   d. silly.

SOMETHING YOU SHOULD KNOW

Group # 2 - African Countries

Nigeria -------This West African country is Africa's most populated country. It is rich with oil.

Kenya --------This beautiful East African country is home for the Gikuyu community. Jomo Kenyatta led them to freedom.

Egypt ---------Civilization began here. It is home of the great pyramids, temples, tombs and King Tut.

Azania -------Sometimes called South Africa, it is a country filled with gold and diamonds. We all must remove apartheid, a form of slavery. Azania is the home of Nelson Mandela.

Tanzania ----It is an East African country and home of the great former President Julius Nyerere.

Group # 3 - African Communities

Ashanti ------A community from Ghana. Many residents work as weavers of beautiful kente cloth and carvers of the Ashanti stool for the king.

Chagga -------A community where the children play among others the same age and are taught to be adults by the time they are 15 years old.

Pondo --------A community where the children learn self-defense at an early age.

Fanti ---------A community in West Africa. They pour libation which is pouring a little wine on the ground to honor their dead family members (ancestors)

Ikoma --------A community in West Africa. They gather honey to eat and sell.

Group # 4 - Black Colleges

Morehouse College ------An all-male school in Atlanta, Georgia. Martin Luther King, Jr. and Spike Lee graduated from Morehouse.

Hampton University --A college in Hampton, Virginia with 4500 students. They have their own radio and TV stations.

Spelman College ------An all-female school with nearly 200 students. It's right next door to Morehouse College. Bill and Camille Cosby gave the school $20 million dollars in 1988.

Tuskegee Institute ----Founded by Booker T. Washington. They have a pre-veterinarian program (animal doctors). It's in Tuskegee, Alabama.

Howard University --One of the largest Black colleges in the country. It's in Washington, D.C. and has its own medical school.

SETCLAE PRONUNCIATION GLOSSARY
(Kiswahili)

Phonics

a-short a	e-long e
i-long i	o-long o
	u-long u

Jambo	Hello
Habari Gani	What is the news?
Njema	Fine
Asante	Thank you
Asante Sana	Thank you very much
Mama	Mother
Baba	Father
Ndada	Sister
Ndugu	Brother
Watoto	Children
Mtoto	Child
Mwalimu	Teacher
Mwanafunzi	Student
Shule	School
Yebo	Yes
La	No
Acha	Stop
Nisamehe	Excuse me
Tafadali	Please
Mzuri	Good
Harambee	Let's pull together
Pamoja Tutashinda	Together we will win
Mzee	Elder
Chakula	Food
Choo	Toilet
Hodi hodi	Hurry
Tutaonana	Goodbye

Moja	One
Mbili	Two
Tatu	Three
Nne	Four
Tano	Five
Sita	Six
Saba	Seven
Nane	Eight
Tisa	Nine
Kumi	Ten

ANSWER KEY

HARAMBEE TIME #3

1. B
2. S
3. B
4. S
5. H

HARAMBEE TIME #6

1. writer
2. lawyer
3. musician
4. scientist
5. athlete
6. teacher

HARAMBEE TIME #9

1. chocolate
2. coffee
3. licorice
4. peach
5. cinnamon
6. copper
7. tan
8. brown

HARAMBEE TIME #12

EGYPT IS IN AFRICA!

HARAMBEE TIME #15

1. C
2. E
3. A
4. B
5. D

HARAMBEE TIME #16

history, past, mistakes, lived,
felt, teach, great

HARAMBEE TIME #17

1. F
2. H
3. J
4. I
5. B
6. C
7. A
8. E
9. G
10. D

HARAMBEE TIME #18

1. peas
2. cloth
3. music
4. Kiswahili (Swahili)
5. you

HARAMBEE TIME #24

1. share
2. kind
3. money
4. love
5. respect